# TWO
# *Little Nuns*

cartoons by

## Bill O'Malley

published by About Comics, Camarillo, California

*Two Little Nuns*
Originally published by *Extension Magazine*, October, 1950
About Comics edition published April, 2018

Customized editions available

Send all queries to *questions@aboutcomics.com*

Bill O'Malley

*"It looks like 'out at third base' to me."*

Bill O'Malley

Bill O'Malley

*"Ah, the belles of Saint Mary's."*

*"Just another thing we can be thankful for, Sister."*

"Well, well, so this is Patrick. You were right, Katie, he is out of this world."

"Enough of Ben Franklin . . ."

*"Too much starch!"*

BILL O'MALLEY

"Just the negative, please; we want to see ourselves in white."

*"Psst! Hey, fellers—Guns!"*

*"You know, Sister, I believe 'sitting in the corner' has lost its effectiveness since we moved into our new building."*

BILL O'MALLEY

*"No chairs, I got the idea at the local drug store."*

"You were speaking of miracles, Sister . . ."

Bill O'Malley

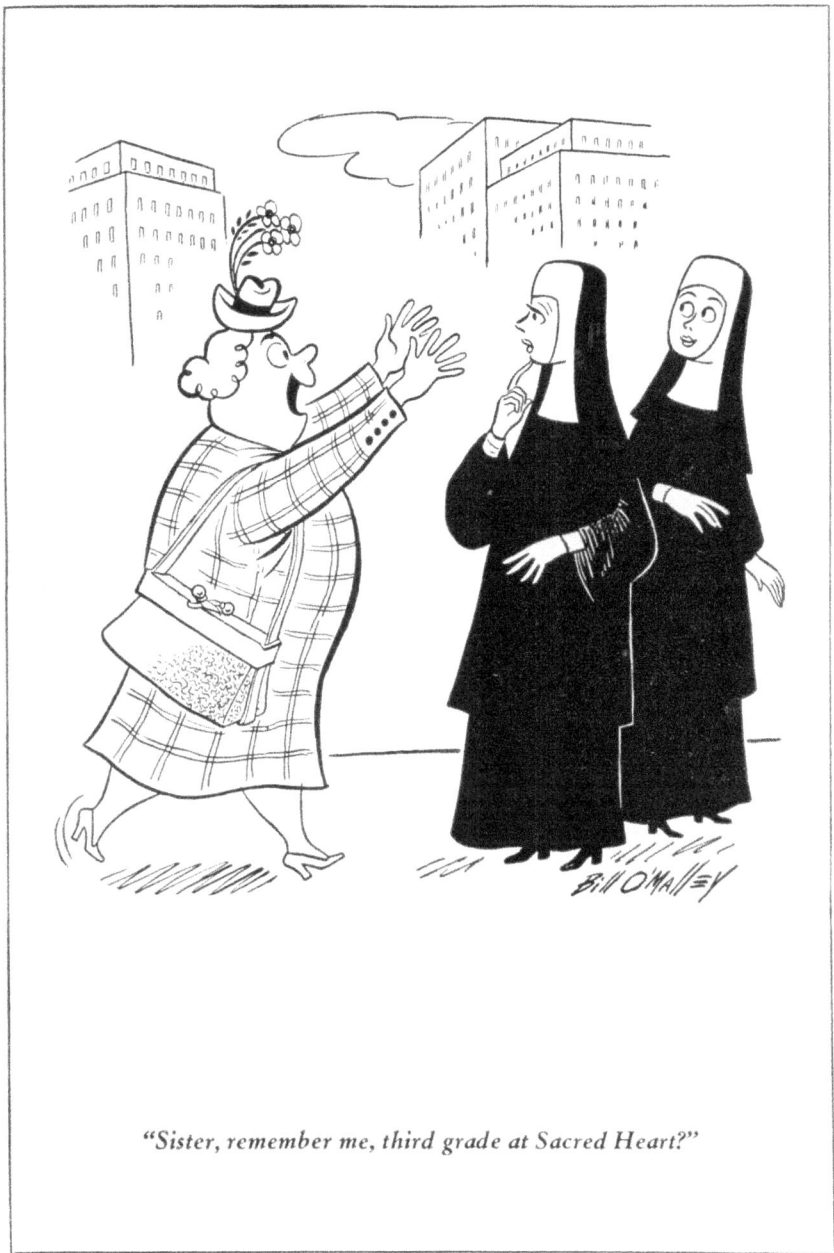

*"Sister, remember me, third grade at Sacred Heart?"*

*"I beg to differ, Ump!"*

*"Mine is the green one with 'Merry Christmas' on it."*

"Why was school closed today, Sister?"

"Hurry, Sister, it's Willie, he——"

"——found a snake!"

Bill O'Malley

Bill O'Malley

"Oh, it's some homework from the home economics class I must go over."

"Look, Mommy! Their bibs haven't any bunnies on 'em like mine!"

"I'll drive—you pray!"

Bill O'Malley

Bill O'Malley

*"I beg your pardon, sir, but how long has it been since you've had your eyes examined?"*

*"Let's not sit behind them!"*

"Just ten minutes more and they'll be out."

"*Father used to be with the air force.*"

Bill O'Malley

Bill O'Malley

*"Doesn't he look like Father Quinn?"*

"*Psst!*"

Bill O'Malley

"There, Father, you can see the school from here."

*"Anyone we know?"*

Bill O'Malley

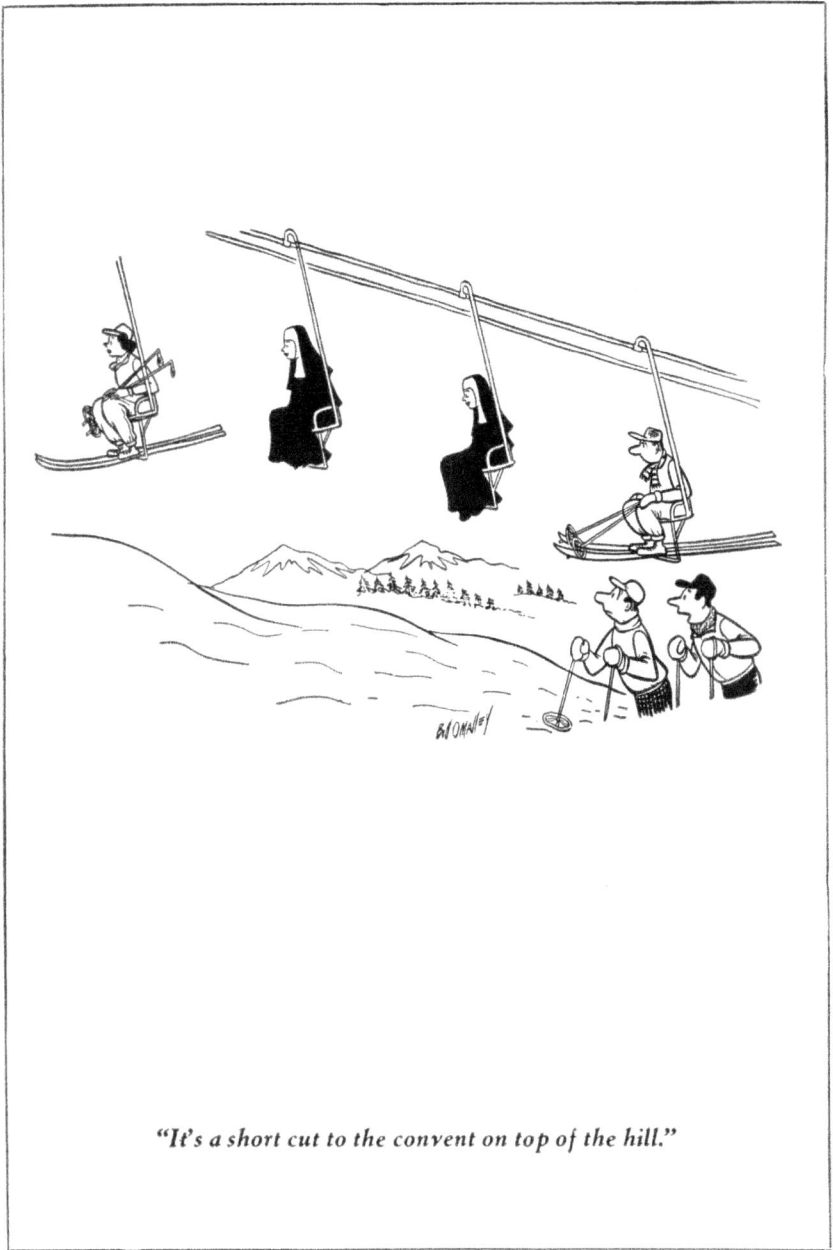

*"It's a short cut to the convent on top of the hill."*

Bill O'Malley

"... *Seven with onions ... six without ... four with mustard ...*
*five with relish but without onions ... three just plain ... and eight*
*with the works!*"

*"Yeah?" "Yeah!"*

"Now before you give this to your Dad, Timmy, you'd better mow the lawn, bring in the firewood, tidy up your room and run the errands."

*"The note must be in my other pocket."*

*"Oh, well, we had to lose one sometime, men."*

*"Cheer up, fellows, we can't win them all."*

*"Chin up."*

"Remember me, Sister, Willie in the Sixth Grade?"

"Now remember?"

Bill O'Malley

"Beaver!"

"Skates! What a marvelous idea!"

CHATTER
CHIRP
CHATTER
CHIRP
CHATTER
CHATTER
CHIRP
CHATTER
SILENCE
Bill O'Malley

"Do you mind the open window, Sisters?"

*"Talk to them, Sister, you're the natural history teacher!"*

"I didn't have the heart to tell him we were leaving."

"*Geraldine Reynolds! I hope your answers here are better than they were in school.*"

"There, that's fine now children . . . let's put our little pets back in their jars . . . and we'll get along with our lesson."

BILL O'MALLEY

"I never know who it's going to be."

"Oh, Mary!"

"Class, we will now . . ."

". . . have a rest period."

*"Sister, would you like to go for a ride . . . oh, skip it!"*

Also available: books of Joe Lane's nun cartoons
*Our Little Nuns*
*More Little Nuns*
*Nuns So Lovable*
*Vale of Dears*
*Yes, Sister! No, Sister!*

or get

**Nun Funnies!**
a lifetime supply all in one volume!

Look for them where you got this book,
or visit www.AboutComics.com

# Classic Cartoon Collections!

Sam Brier's 1950s quirky comic strip is about kids playing as adults... or adults drawn as kids.

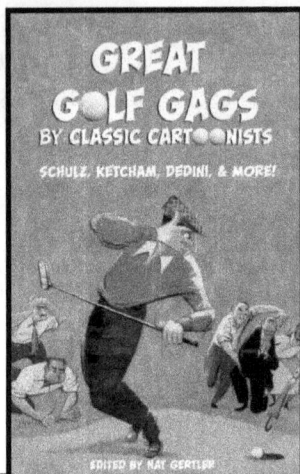

Golf cartoons by Hank Ketcham, Eldon Dedini, Virgil Partch, Bill O'Malley, & more

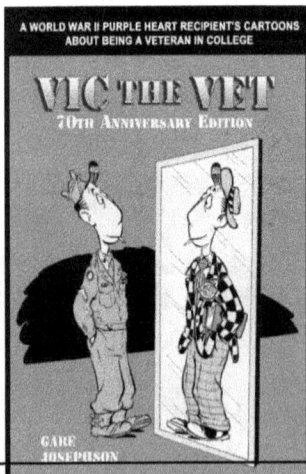

Cartoons about being a World War II vet at college on the GI Bill... by a World War II vet while at college.

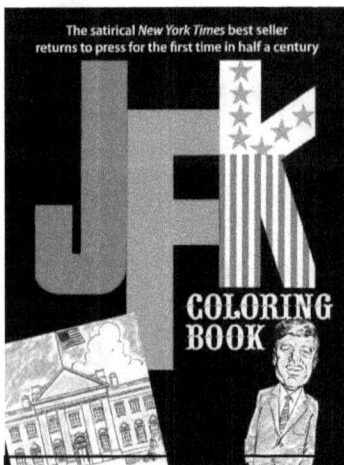

Mort Drucker illustrates this New York Times best-seller